My First Animal Library

Gazelles

by Penelope S. Nelson

Bullfrog Books

Ideas for Parents and Teachers

Bullfrog Books let children practice reading informational text at the earliest reading levels. Repetition, familiar words, and photo labels support early readers.

Before Reading

- Discuss the cover photo. What does it tell them?

- Look at the picture glossary together. Read and discuss the words.

Read the Book

- "Walk" through the book and look at the photos. Let the child ask questions. Point out the photo labels.

- Read the book to the child, or have him or her read independently.

After Reading

- Prompt the child to think more. Ask: What did you know about gazelles before reading this book? What more would you like to learn about them after reading it?

Bullfrog Books are published by Jump!
5357 Penn Avenue South
Minneapolis, MN 55419
www.jumplibrary.com

Copyright © 2020 Jump! International copyright reserved in all countries. No part of this book may be reproduced in any form without written permission from the publisher.

Library of Congress Cataloging-in-Publication Data

Names: Nelson, Penelope, 1994– author.
Title: Gazelles / by Penelope S. Nelson.
Description: Bullfrog books edition.
Minneapolis, MN : Jump!, Inc., [2020]
Series: My first animal library
Audience: Age 5–8. | Audience: K to Grade 3.
Includes index.
Identifiers: LCCN 2018037654 (print)
LCCN 2018039062 (ebook)
ISBN 9781641285537 (ebook)
ISBN 9781641285520 (hardcover : alk. paper)
Subjects: LCSH: Gazelles—Juvenile literature.
Classification: LCC QL737.U53 (ebook)
LCC QL737.U53 N45 2019 (print)
DDC 599.64/69—dc23
LC record available at https://lccn.loc.gov/2018037654

Editor: Jenna Trnka
Designer: Jenna Casura

Photo Credits: WLDavies/iStock, cover; KenCanning/iStock, 1; stockphoto mania/Shutterstock, 3; TT/iStock, 4; Bebedi/iStock, 5, 23tm; skilpad/iStock, 6–7, 23bm; Friedrich von Horsten/Alamy, 8–9, 23tr; Ignacio Palacios/Getty, 10, 14–15; GlobalP/iStock, 11, 23bl; Adam Jones/Getty, 12–13; TTphoto/Shutterstock, 16–17; Franz Wogerer/Getty, 18; Laura Romin & Larry Dalton/Alamy, 19; Dennis W Donohue/Shutterstock, 20–21, 23tl; Volodymyr Burdiak/Shutterstock, 22; rsooll/Shutterstock, 23br; JackF/iStock, 24.

Printed in the United States of America at Corporate Graphics in North Mankato, Minnesota.

Table of Contents

Fast Runners

It is morning.

A gazelle grazes.
On what? Grass.

5

Gazelles live in dry areas.

Food can be hard to find.

The herd travels together.

It roams large areas
to look for food.

herd

They hear a predator!

What is it?

A lion? Crocodile?

It is a cheetah!

Run!

Gazelles have long legs.

They are fast!

They are safe.

They go back
to eating.

They get water
from plants.

Grass. Shoots.
Leaves, too.

Males have long horns.

horns

For what?
Fighting.

Moms have one or two fawns.

They live with the herd.

They will grow up!

fawn

Parts of a Gazelle

horns
All male gazelles have horns. Some females do, too. They may be long and twisted. They may be short. Some are striped!

ears
Large ears listen for predators.

nose
Gazelles have a good sense of smell. This helps them smell nearby predators.

legs
Long legs help gazelles run fast. They can run up to 60 miles (97 kilometers) per hour.

hooves
Gazelles are hooved animals.

Picture Glossary

fawns
Young gazelles.

grazes
Feeds on growing plants.

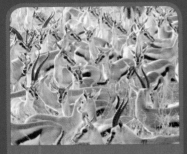

herd
A group that lives and travels together.

predator
An animal that hunts other animals for food.

roams
Wanders through an area.

shoots
New or young plants.

Index

To Learn More

Finding more information is as easy as 1, 2, 3.

❶ Go to www.factsurfer.com

❷ Enter "gazelles" into the search box.

❸ Click the "Surf" button to see a list of websites.

24